Sight Word Stories & Seatwork Activities 1

REM 136A

A TEACHING RESOURCE FROM...

©1988, 1997, 1998, 2000
**Copyright by Remedia Publications, Inc.
All Rights Reserved. Printed in the U.S.A.**

The purchase of this unit entitles the individual teacher to reproduce copies for classroom use. The reproduction of any part for an entire school or school system is strictly prohibited.

To find Remedia products in a store near you, contact:
www.rempub.com/stores

REMEDIA PUBLICATIONS   10135 E. VIA LINDA   #D124   SCOTTSDALE, AZ 85258

TO THE TEACHER:

<u>Sight Word Stories and Seatwork Activities</u> is a collection of stories which utilize a list of nouns most commonly found in beginning readers. Each lesson is based on three or four nouns woven into a short story with seven related seatwork activities.

How To Use These Materials

Once the student is familiar with the procedure for completing each lesson, he or she can then complete subsequent lessons in the same manner.

Story:

The key nouns are highlighted in a box. The teacher may wish to introduce each word by pronouncing it for the students and elaborating by asking students to relate their own experiences with the word.

Questions:

Each story has several questions related to the content of the story just read.

Scanning:

Scanning is a reading skill which beginning readers can develop. They simply focus on a key word and count how many times that word appears in the story. (For purposes of consistency, students should count key words occurring in the title of the story, but not in the word box.)

Completion:

In this activity, students are given sentences with one word missing. The missing words are located in a list next to the sentences.

Choose the Word:

Students are presented with sentences that relate to the story. They must choose one of two words to complete the sentence properly, according to the story.

Sequencing:

This activity is a comprehension check of students' ability to remember the events in the story in correct sequence. Students indicate which event occurred first by numbering 1, 2, 3.

Yes/No:

This activity consists of sentences which do not necessarily relate to the story. The student indicates whether or not the sentence makes sense or could happen by writing "yes" or "no" in the blank following the sentence. For purposes of consistency in answering the questions, instruct the students to respond to the statements by writing "yes" if it could really happen, whether or not it happened in the story, and vice versa. For example, in many of the stories, animals are able to talk. However, if the student encountered a statement that said, "A cat can talk," they should answer it "no," because in real life cats do not talk.

Following Directions:

The final activity involves reading simple instructions and carrying out the directions. In most cases, this involves drawing an object, coloring it a specific color, and locating it in a certain place. The student is also given an opportunity to be creative by imagining what someone or something would say in the situation they just created.

Name _____

| baby |
| airplane |
| mother |

The Baby and the Airplane

One day a baby saw a big, blue airplane.

The baby said, "I want to go for a ride on the big airplane."

She got into the airplane. The airplane did not go. The airplane had no gas in it.

The mother went to look for the baby.

"Come here!" said the mother.

The mother got the baby out of the airplane. The mother said, "I will get you a little airplane, baby. No big airplanes for you."

QUESTIONS:

1. What is the name of the story?
   _____
2. What color was the big airplane? _____
3. Was the airplane big or little? _____
4. Was the baby a boy or a girl? _____
5. Who went to look for the baby? _____
6. What will the mother get for the baby? _____

SCANNING:

1. baby ____   3. airplanes ____
2. airplane ____   4. mother ____

STORY #1

Name _____

COMPLETION:

1. This is an _____.

2. This is a _____.

3. I can go for a _____.

4. The airplane is _____.

5. A baby is _____.

6. The baby has a _____.

| big |
| baby |
| airplane |
| little |
| ride |
| mother |

CHOOSE THE WORD:

1. One day a _____ saw an airplane.
                baby   **boy**

2. The baby got _____ the airplane.
                into   **out**

3. The _____ went to look for the baby.
                mother   **father**

4. The mother will get the baby a _____ airplane.
                little   **big**

SEQUENCING: (1   2   3)

_____ The mother got the baby out of the airplane.

_____ The baby got into the airplane.

_____ The baby saw an airplane.

STORY #1

Name _____

YES/NO:

1. A baby can fly. _____
2. An airplane can fly. _____
3. An airplane can be blue. _____
4. A mother can have a baby. _____
5. A baby can have a mother. _____
6. An airplane can have a mother. _____
7. A baby is little. _____
8. An airplane can be big. _____
9. An airplane can be little. _____
10. A mother can fly. _____
11. A baby can be a boy. _____
12. A baby can be a girl. _____
13. A baby can be an airplane. _____
14. You can ride in an airplane. _____

FOLLOWING DIRECTIONS:

1. Draw an airplane.
2. Color the airplane red.
3. Draw a baby on the airplane.
4. Color the baby green.
5. What is the baby saying?

STORY #1

Name _____

bird
basket
apple
bell
boy

The Bird and the Basket

One day a little, red bird saw a brown basket.

The red bird said, "What is in the basket? I will go and see."

The bird went to the brown basket. The bird took the top off the basket. In the basket, the bird saw a big, red apple and a little bell.

The bird said, "I want that red apple."

But when the bird got the apple, the bell went: RING, RING, RING!

Then a boy came up to the bird. "That is MY apple," said the boy. "Go away, bird."

The bird did not get the apple. The bird did not get the bell. The bird did not get the basket.

But, the bird did get something.

QUESTIONS:

1. What color was the bird? _____
2. What color was the basket? _____
3. What was in the basket?
   an _____ and a _____
4. What is the name of the story?
   _____
5. Did the bird get the apple? _____
6. Who got the apple? _____

STORY #2

Name _____

SCANNING:

1. bird _____   4. bell _____

2. basket _____   5. boy _____

3. apple _____

COMPLETION:

1. This is a _____ .

2. A _____ can fly.

3. An apple is _____ .

4. This is a _____ .

5. The _____ can eat an apple.

basket
bird
bell
red
boy

CHOOSE THE WORD:

1. A bird saw a _____ basket.
                    brown   **red**

2. The bird took the _____ off the basket.
                    apple   **top**

3. A little _____ was in the basket.
                    bell   **airplane**

4. A _____ came up to the bird.
                    girl   **boy**

5. The bird _____ get the apple.
                    did not   **did**

STORY #2

Name _____

SEQUENCING: (1 2 3)

_____ The bell went: RING, RING, RING.

_____ The boy came up to the bird.

_____ The bird went to the basket.

YES/NO:

1. A bird can fly.   _____
2. A basket can fly.   _____
3. A bird can be red.   _____
4. A basket can be brown.   _____
5. A bird can be brown.   _____
6. A boy can fly.   _____
7. An apple can fly.   _____
8. An apple can be red.   _____
9. An apple can be in a basket.   _____
10. A boy can be in an apple.   _____

FOLLOWING DIRECTIONS:

1. Draw a basket.
2. Color the basket blue.
3. Draw a bird on the basket.
4. Draw a boy near the bird.
5. What is the bird saying?

STORY #2

Name _____

| boy |
| barn |
| box |
| dad |

The Box In the Barn

A boy went to play in a big, red barn. He went into the barn. He saw a box.

The boy said, "What is in the box?"

The boy could not get the box open. He said, "What can I do? I will get my dad."

The boy got his dad. His dad went to the barn with the boy. His dad got the box open.

In the box was something that made the boy happy. It made his dad happy, too.

The boy said, "Let's go play with this."

QUESTIONS:

1. Who went to play in the barn? _____
2. What was in the barn? _____
3. Who could not open the box? _____
4. Who did open the box? _____
5. What was in the box? _____
   a barn?   a ball?   a boy?

SCANNING:

1. box ____   2. barn ____   3. dad ____   4. boy ____

STORY #3

Name _____

COMPLETION:

1. The boy is _____ .

2. The dad can _____ the box.

3. The _____ is red.

4. What is in the _____ ?

5. The boy's _____ went to the barn.

dad
box
barn
open
happy

CHOOSE THE WORD:

1. A boy went to play in a _____ .
                      bell   **barn**

2. A _____ was in the barn.
      dog   **box**

3. The boy went to _____ his dad.
                     get   **eat**

4. A _____ was in the box.
      bell   **ball**

SEQUENCING: (1 2 3)

_____ A boy went to a barn.

_____ His dad got the box open.

_____ The boy could not open the box.

STORY #3

Name _____

YES/NO:

1. A bird can be red. _____
2. A barn can be red. _____
3. A box can be in a barn. _____
4. A barn can be in a box. _____
5. A boy can be in a box. _____
6. A barn can be in a boy. _____
7. A box can be open. _____
8. A barn can be open. _____
9. A man can get a box. _____
10. A man can open a box. _____
11. A boy can be a box. _____
12. A boy can be happy. _____
13. A box can be happy. _____

FOLLOWING DIRECTIONS:

1. Draw a box.
2. Color the box green.
3. Draw something by the box that would make a boy happy.

9

STORY #3

Name _____

| bear |
| bed |
| sleep |

The Bear and His Bed

A big, brown bear had a big bed. He liked to sleep in his big bed. One night he got into his bed. He could not sleep.

The bear sat up. There was something in his bed.

"What is in this bed?" asked the bear.

The bear got up. He looked in his bed. He found something.

The bear said, "I can eat this. Then I can get into bed and go to sleep," and he did.

QUESTIONS:

1. What is the name of this story?
   _____

2. What did the bear like to do?
   _____

3. When did the bear get into his bed? _____

4. Where did he look for something? _____

5. What was in his bed? a baby?   a ball?   an apple?
   _____

SCANNING:

1. bear _____   2. _____   3. sleep _____

STORY #4

Name _____

COMPLETION:

1. I sleep in my _____ at night.
2. I can _____ in a bed.
3. I like to _____ apples.
4. I see a big, brown _____ .
5. In the _____ , I go to school.
6. I sleep at _____ .

```
bear
bed
sleep
eat
night
day
```

CHOOSE THE WORD:

1. The bear had a _____ bed.
   big   **little**

2. One _____ , he got into his bed.
   day   **night**

3. He could not _____ .
   sleep   **eat**

4. The bear said, "I can _____ this."
   sleep   **eat**

5. An _____ was in the bed.
   apple   **airplane**

SEQUENCING: (1 2 3)

____ The bear looked for something in his bed.

____ The bear went to sleep.

____ The bear got into his bed.

11   STORY #4

Name _____

YES/NO:

1. You can sleep in a bear. _____
2. You can sleep in a bed. _____
3. You can eat a bed. _____
4. You can eat in a bed. _____
5. A boy can eat at night. _____
6. A bear can eat an apple. _____
7. A bear can sleep at night. _____
8. An apple can sleep. _____
9. A bear can be brown. _____
10. An airplane can sleep. _____
11. A boy can sleep on an airplane. _____
12. A bear can fly an airplane. _____

FOLLOWING DIRECTIONS:

1. Draw a bed.
2. Draw a boy in the bed.
3. Color the bed red.
4. Color the boy yellow.
5. What is the boy dreaming about?

STORY #4

Name _____

girl
birthday
cake
piece

The Birthday Cake

A girl had a birthday. Her mother made her a big birthday cake.

The cake was good. The girl liked the cake very, very, very, very much. The girl ate one big piece of cake. Then, she ate one more big piece of cake. Then, she ate one more big piece of cake.

Then, she got sick.

Her mother said, "You can go to bed now, little girl. This will not be a good birthday for you if you are sick."

The girl said, "This is a good birthday. But the cake was a little too good."

QUESTIONS:

1. Who made the birthday cake? _____
2. Was the cake good? _____
3. How many pieces of cake did the girl eat? _____
4. How did the girl feel? _____
5. Was it a good birthday? _____
6. What is the name of the story?
_____

SCANNING:

1. piece ____
2. birthday ____
3. cake ____
4. girl ____

Name _____

COMPLETION:

1. I like to eat _____ .

2. The girl got _____ .

3. The cake is _____ good.

4. Today is my _____ .

5. The girl _____ the cake.

6. You are a _____ girl.

| birthday |
| cake |
| good |
| very |
| sick |
| ate |

CHOOSE THE WORD:

1. A _____ had a birthday.
         boy   **girl**

2. Her _____ made her a birthday cake.
      father   **mother**

3. The girl liked the _____ very much.
         cake   **cat**

4. The girl got _____ .
         sick   **sad**

5. The cake was a little too _____ .
         bad   **good**

SEQUENCING: (1 2 3)

____ The girl got sick.

____ The girl had a birthday.

____ The girl ate too much cake.

STORY #5

Name _____

YES/NO:

1. A girl can have a birthday. _____
2. A girl can get sick. _____
3. A cake can get sick. _____
4. A girl can be good. _____
5. A cake can be good. _____
6. A mother can get sick. _____
7. A mother can have a birthday. _____
8. A cake can eat a boy. _____
9. A boy can eat a cake. _____
10. A cake can be a mother. _____
11. A cake can be brown. _____
12. A cake can have a birthday. _____

FOLLOWING DIRECTIONS:

1. Draw a cake.
2. Make it a birthday cake.
3. Color the cake pink.
4. Who will eat the cake?

Name _____

| boat |
| book |
| paper |

The Boat Book

A boy had a book about boats. He liked to read about boats. He liked to play with boats. He liked to make boats. He liked all boats.

The book had a story about how to make a boat out of paper. The boy got some paper. Then, he made a boat.

The boy said, "This is a good book. It is my boat book. The book is not a boat, but the book can help me make a boat."

QUESTIONS:

1. What was the book about? _____
2. Did the boy like to make boats? _____
3. What did the boy get to make a boat? _____
4. Did the boy make a car? _____
5. Did the boy like the book? _____
6. What is the name of the story? _____

_____

SCANNING:

1. boat _____   3. boats _____
2. book _____   4. paper _____

STORY #6

Name _____

COMPLETION:

1. This is a _____ book to read.
2. The boat is made of _____ .
3. I can read a _____ .
4. I like to _____ about boats.
5. The boy can _____ a paper boat.
6. The _____ is on the water.

boat
book
make
paper
read
good

CHOOSE THE WORD:

1. A boy had a _____ about boats.
           book   **box**

2. He liked to _____ with boats.
         ride   **play**

3. The book told how to make a _____ boat.
         paper   **books**

4. The boy said the book was _____ .
         bad   **good**

SEQUENCING: (1 2 3)

_____ A boy had a book about boats.

_____ The boy got some paper.

_____ The boy made a paper boat.

17

STORY #6

Name _____

YES/NO:

1. A boy can ride in a book. _____
2. A boat can be blue. _____
3. A girl can read a boat. _____
4. A boat can be made of paper. _____
5. A book can be made of paper. _____
6. A book can be blue. _____
7. A girl can ride in a boat. _____
8. A boat can fly. _____
9. A book can fly. _____
10. A girl can ride in a book. _____
11. A boat can be big. _____
12. A boat can be little. _____

FOLLOWING DIRECTIONS:

1. Draw a boat.
2. Color the boat orange.
3. Draw a book by the boat.
4. Color the book red.

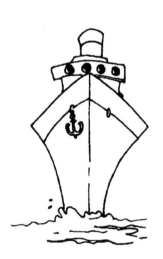

STORY #6

Name _____

| bus |
| cat |
| school |

The Cat on the Bus

A girl had a white cat. She liked her cat.

When the school bus came to take the girl to school, the cat wanted to go, too. But the girl said, "Cat, you do not want to go to school. A cat can not go on the bus."

The girl went to school. The cat did not go to school.

One day, the girl got on the bus. A boy on the bus said, "Look! I see a cat on the bus."

The girl looked. It was her cat.

The girl said, "Cat, you do want to go to school. I guess a cat can go to school on the bus."

QUESTIONS:

1. What is the name of the story?

   _____

2. What color was the cat? _____

3. Where did the cat want to go? _____

4. Who saw the cat on the bus? _____

5. Can the cat ride the bus? _____

SCANNING:

1. bus _____   2. white _____   3. cat _____   4. school _____

Name _____

COMPLETION:

1. The cat _____ to go to school.

2. The boys and girls ride on a _____ .

3. The cat is _____ .

4. The _____ rode on the bus.

5. Children go to _____ .

| cat |
| bus |
| school |
| white |
| wants |

CHOOSE THE WORD:

1. The girl had a _____ cat.
               black   **white**

2. The cat wanted to go to _____ .
          school   **home**

3. The _____ came for the girl.
      car   **bus**

4. The _____ got on the bus.
      cat   **dog**

5. The cat went to _____ .
        sing   **school**

SEQUENCING: (1 2 3)

_____ A cat wanted to go to school.

_____ The cat got on the bus.

_____ The bus came for the girl.

STORY #7

Name _____

YES/NO:

1. A girl can ride on a bus. _____
2. A boy can go to school on a bus. _____
3. A cat can be white. _____
4. A cat can be green. _____
5. A girl can ride a cat. _____
6. A boy can ride a bus. _____
7. A girl can play with a cat. _____
8. A bus can play with a cat. _____
9. A bus can be blue. _____
10. A bus can eat. _____
11. A boy can eat. _____
12. A cat can eat. _____

FOLLOWING DIRECTIONS:

1. Draw a bus.
2. Color the bus blue.
3. Draw a girl next to the bus.
4. The girl is not going to school.
5. What is the girl saying?

Name _____

chicken
bread
fox

The Chicken and the Bread

A yellow chicken liked to eat bread. She ate bread all day long. She ate white bread. She ate dark bread. She ate and ate the bread.

A fox saw the chicken. The fox said, "I would like to eat, too. I would like to eat that chicken. I will eat the chicken after the chicken eats a lot of bread."

The chicken ate and ate. She got very fat.

The fox went up to the chicken. The fox said, "Chicken, I would like to eat you."

The chicken said, "Fox, eat some bread. It is very good."

The fox ate the bread. Then, he did not want to eat the chicken. The fox and the chicken ate the bread, and they were both happy.

QUESTIONS:

1. What did the chicken like to eat? _____

2. Who saw the chicken? _____

3. What did the chicken give the fox? _____

4. Did the fox eat the chicken? _____

5. Did the fox eat the bread? _____

6. What is the name of the story?

_____

Name _____

SCANNING:

1. fox _____   3. chicken _____

2. bread _____   4. ate _____

COMPLETION:

1. I see a yellow _____ in the barn.

2. I like to _____ bread.

3. The chicken _____ some bread.

4. This is a _____ .

5. The _____ chicken ate a lot of bread.

ate
fat
fox
eat
chicken

CHOOSE THE WORD:

1. A _____ chicken liked to eat bread.
         red   yellow

2. One day a _____ saw the chicken.
         dog   fox

3. The fox wanted to _____ the chicken.
         eat   see

4. The chicken got very _____ .
         fat   funny

5. The chicken gave the fox some _____ .
         bread   meat

6. The fox _____ eat the chicken.
         did   did not

STORY #8

Name _____

SEQUENCING: (1 2 3)

_____ A fox wanted to eat the chicken.

_____ A chicken ate bread.

_____ The chicken gave the fox some bread.

YES/NO:

1. A boy can eat bread.   _____

2. A boy can eat chicken.   _____

3. A boy can be a fox.   _____

4. A fox can be fat.   _____

5. A chicken can live in a barn.   _____

6. A girl goes to school.   _____

7. A chicken goes to school.   _____

8. A fox has four feet.   _____

9. A chicken has four feet.   _____

10. A boy has two feet.   _____

FOLLOWING DIRECTIONS:

1. Draw a little fox.   2. Draw a big chicken.   3. What is the chicken saying?

STORY #8

Name _____

| boy |
| cap |
| puppy |
| ball |

The Boy and the Cap

A boy went to play ball with his friends. He had on his blue cap. He liked to play ball.

His friend made the ball go very far. The boy went to get the ball, but his blue cap fell off. It fell by a puppy.

The puppy got the cap and ran, ran, ran. The boy ran after the puppy.

The boy said, "Puppy! Give me the cap!" But the puppy did not stop.

The boy got the ball and said, "Puppy! Get the ball!"

The puppy went to get the ball and left the cap. The boy said, "I have the cap — but I want the ball now!"

QUESTIONS:

1. What color was the cap? _____
2. Where did the cap fall? _____
3. What did the puppy do with the cap? _____
4. What did the boy give the puppy? _____
5. What did the boy want then? _____
6. What is the name of the story? _____

STORY #9

Name _____

SCANNING:

1. puppy _____   3. boy _____
2. ball _____   4. cap _____

COMPLETION:

| boy |
| cap |
| puppy |
| ball |
| friend |
| like |

1. I _____ to play ball.
2. The _____ on my head is blue.
3. My _____ and I like to play.
4. My little _____ likes to run.
5. I am not a girl; I am a _____.
6. Throw me the _____.

CHOOSE THE WORD:

1. A boy went to play _____ with his friends.
                                    ball   cap
2. He had on his _____ cap.
                         red   blue
3. The cap fell by a _____.
                        puppy   cat
4. The puppy _____ away with the cap.
                        run   ran
5. The boy gave the puppy a _____.
                        ball   bell
6. The puppy left the _____.
                        cap   bell

STORY #9

Name _____

SEQUENCING: (1 2 3)

_____ The puppy ran away with the cap.

_____ The boy ran after the puppy to get the cap.

_____ The boy went to play ball.

YES/NO:

1. A puppy can run. _____

2. A cap can run. _____

3. A puppy can run after a cap. _____

4. A cap can run after a boy. _____

5. A boy can be a friend. _____

6. A puppy can be a friend. _____

7. A ball can be blue. _____

8. A puppy can be blue. _____

9. A cap can be blue. _____

10. A boy can have a blue cap. _____

FOLLOWING DIRECTIONS:

1. Draw a cap.
2. Color the cap blue.
3. Draw a ball.
4. Circle the one that a boy will play with if he has a friend at his house.
5. What game would they play?

STORY #9

Name _____

| man |
| men |
| car |
| grass |
| green |
| street |

The Green Car

A man had a big, green car. He liked to drive his car on the grass.

One day, some men came up to the man and said, "You can not drive your car on the grass!"

The man said, "My car is green. I like to drive it on the green grass. It is fun."

The men said, "If you drive your car on the green grass, it will not be green any more. We will make it black. We have something here to make your green car into a black car."

The man said, "I do not want a black car. I will drive my car on the street, not the grass."

The men said, "Good. Your car will stay green."

QUESTIONS:

1. What is the name of the story?
   _____

2. What color was the car? _____

3. Where did the man drive his car? _____

4. Who was mad at the man? _____

5. What color did they want to make his car? _____

6. Where does the man drive his car now? _____

STORY #10

Name _____

SCANNING:

1. man _____   4. grass _____

2. men _____   5. street _____

3. car _____   6. green _____

COMPLETION:

1. You should _____ drive on the grass.

2. Two _____ walked on the street.

3. Do you like my new green _____ ?

4. My dad is a _____ .

5. The big car went down the _____ .

6. I do not know how to _____ a car.

| drive |
| men |
| man |
| car |
| street |
| not |

CHOOSE THE WORD:

1. The man had a _____ green car.
       little   big

2. He liked to drive on the _____ .
              grass   street

3. Some _____ did not want the man to
       children   men

   drive on the _____ .
              grass   table

4. The man did not want a _____ car.
                 green   black

29   STORY #10

Name _____

SEQUENCING: (1 2 3)

_____ A man liked to drive on the grass.

_____ Some men did not want the car on the grass.

_____ The man did not drive on the grass any more.

YES/NO:

1. A man can drive a car. _____
2. A car can drive a man. _____
3. A car can go on the street. _____
4. A man can walk on the grass. _____
5. A car can walk on the grass. _____
6. A cat can walk on the grass. _____
7. A cat can walk on a car. _____
8. A car can be black. _____
9. A street can be black. _____
10. A man can make a car black. _____

FOLLOWING DIRECTIONS:

1. Draw a car.
2. Draw two men by the car.
3. Color the car black.
4. What are the men saying about the car?

Name _____

children
class
funny
coat
joke

The Children and Their Coats

One day, the children in a class at school wanted to play a funny joke. The children each took a coat that was not the right coat.

A girl took the coat from a boy. One tall boy took the coat from a short boy. One girl took a coat that was too big. They said, "This joke is very funny."

The mothers came to school to get the children. One mother wanted a boy in a boy's coat. Another mother wanted a tall girl in a tall girl's coat. The children all had on funny coats.

The mothers said, "We can not go home with our children if our children do not have the right coats."

The children said, "This was funny, but now it is time to go home."

So the girls put on the girls' coats. The boys put on the boys' coats. The tall children put on tall coats and the short children put on short coats.

Then the mothers went home with the right children and the right coats.

QUESTIONS:

1. What is the name of the story?

   _____

2. What did the children want to play? _____

3. The children said, "This was _____ , but now it is time to go _____ ."

STORY #11

Name _____

SCANNING:

1. children _____   4. coats _____

2. class _____   5. joke _____

3. coat _____   6. funny _____

COMPLETION:

1. Many _____ went for a walk.

2. Let's play a _____ on the boy.

3. The children in my _____ are nice.

4. Put on your _____ .

5. This is the _____ coat for me.

6. My mother is very _____ .

| class |
| children |
| joke |
| coat |
| tall |
| right |

CHOOSE THE WORD:

1. The children wanted to _____ a joke.
         read   **play**

2. One girl took a coat from a _____ .
         girl   **boy**

3. A tall boy took a coat from a _____ boy.
         tall   **short**

4. The children said it was very _____ .
         sad   **funny**

5. The _____ wanted the right coats.
         mothers   **fathers**

STORY #11

Name _____

SEQUENCING: (1 2 3)

_____ The children put on the right coats.

_____ The children wanted to play a joke.

_____ The mothers came to get the children.

YES/NO:

1. Children can wear coats.   _____

2. A dog can wear a coat.   _____

3. A joke can be funny.   _____

4. A coat can be red.   _____

5. A boy can wear a coat.   _____

6. Boys and girls are children.   _____

7. Boy and girls can be in a class.   _____

8. Dogs are children.   _____

9. Dogs like children.   _____

10. A class can be at a school.   _____

FOLLOWING DIRECTIONS:

1. Draw a tall girl with a short coat.   3. What is the girl saying?
2. Draw a short boy with a tall coat.   4. What is the boy saying?

STORY #11

Name _____

| corn |
| cow |
| dog |
| road |
| farm |

Corn on the Road

A cow and a dog were looking for something to eat.

The cow said, "I want some cake. Cake would be good."

The dog said, "I like bread. I would like to eat some bread."

They walked down the road. They came to a big farm.

The cow said, "Look! Do you see what I see? Corn! Yellow corn! Good corn! Lots of corn!"

The dog said, "I do not want bread. I want corn."

The cow said, "I do not want cake. I want corn."

They sat down by the farm and ate and ate and ate.

QUESTIONS:

1. What is the name of the story?

   _____

2. What were the cow and the dog looking for?

   _____

3. What did the cow want to eat at first? _____

4. What did the dog want to eat at first? _____

5. What did they see at a farm? _____

STORY #12

Name _____

SCANNING:

1. cow _____
2. corn _____
3. dog _____
4. road _____
5. farm _____

COMPLETION:

1. This is a _____ .
2. I can walk down a _____ .
3. The _____ lives on a farm.
4. The cow can eat some _____ .
5. The corn grows on a _____ .
6. The dog can _____ corn.

dog
eat
road
cow
corn
farm

CHOOSE THE WORD:

1. A cow and a _____ were looking for something to eat.
                    bear   **dog**

2. They walked down the _____ .
                    road   **farm**

3. The _____ saw some yellow corn.
                 cat   **cow**

4. The cow and the dog _____ the corn.
                 read   **ate**

5. Now they did not want cake or _____ .
                 bread   **corn**

Name _____

SEQUENCING: (1 2 3)

_____ The cow and the dog walked down the road.

_____ The cow and the dog wanted something to eat.

_____ The cow and the dog ate corn.

YES/NO:

1. A cow can eat corn.   _____
2. A cow can eat a dog.   _____
3. A dog can eat a cow.   _____
4. A dog can live on a farm.   _____
5. A cow can live on a farm.   _____
6. A boy can live on a farm.   _____
7. A farm can walk down a road.   _____
8. A dog can walk down a road.   _____
9. Corn can walk down a road.   _____
10. You can live by a road.   _____

FOLLOWING DIRECTIONS:

1. Draw a road.
2. Draw a house on the road.
3. Draw a cow near the house.
4. Draw a boy on the road.
5. What is the boy saying?

STORY #12

Answer Key - Sight Word Stories and Seatwork Activities 1

PAGE 1   **Questions:** 1) The Baby and The Airplane 2) blue 3) big 4) girl 5) mother 6) little airplane
  Scanning: 1) 6 2) 8 3) 1 4) 4

PAGE 2   **Completion:** 1) airplane 2) baby 3) ride 4) big 5) little 6) mother   **Choose the Word:** 1) baby 2) into 3) mother 4) little   **Sequencing:** 3-2-1

PAGE 3   **Yes/No:** 1) no 2) yes 3) yes 4) yes 5) yes 6) no 7) yes 8) yes 9) yes 10) no 11) yes 12) yes 13) no 14) yes

PAGE 4   **Questions:** 1) red 2) brown 3) apple, bell 4) The Bird and the Basket 5) no 6) boy

PAGE 5   **Scanning:** 1) 14 2) 7 3) 5 4) 3 5) 2   **Completion:** 1) basket 2) bird 3) red 4) bell 5) boy
  Choose the Word: 1) brown 2) top 3) bell 4) boy 5) did not

PAGE 6   **Sequencing:** 2-3-1   **Yes/No:** 1) yes 2) no 3) yes 4) yes 5) yes 6) no 7) no 8) yes 9) yes 10) no

PAGE 7   **Questions:** 1) boy 2) box 3) boy 4) dad 5) ball   **Scanning:** 1) 6 2) 4 3) 5 4) 7

PAGE 8   **Completion:** 1) happy 2) open 3) barn 4) box 5) dad   **Choose the Word:** 1) barn 2) box 3) get 4) ball
  Sequencing: 1-3-2

PAGE 9   **Yes/No:** 1) yes 2) yes 3) yes 4) no 5) yes 6) no 7) yes 8) yes 9) yes 10) yes 11) no 12) yes 13) no

PAGE 10   **Questions:** 1) The Bear and His Bed 2) sleep 3) one night 4) in the bed 5) apple   **Scanning:** 1) 6 2) 8 3) 3

PAGE 11   **Completion:** 1) bed 2) sleep 3) eat 4) bear 5) day 6) night   **Choose the Word:** 1) big 2) night 3) sleep 4) eat 5) apple   **Sequencing:** 2-3-1

PAGE 12   **Yes/No:** 1) no 2) yes 3) no 4) yes 5) yes 6) yes 7) yes 8) no 9) yes 10) no 11) yes 12) no

PAGE 13   **Questions:** 1) mother 2) yes 3) three 4) sick 5) yes 6) The Birthday Cake   **Scanning:** 1) 3 2) 5 3) 8 4) 5

PAGE 14   **Completion:** 1) cake 2) sick 3) very 4) birthday 5) ate 6) good   **Choose the Word:** 1) girl 2) mother 3) cake 4) sick 5) good   **Sequencing:** 3-1-2

PAGE 15   **Yes/No:** 1) yes 2) yes 3) no 4) yes 5) yes 6) yes 7) yes 8) no 9) yes 10) no 11) yes 12) no

PAGE 16   **Questions:** 1) boats 2) yes 3) paper 4) no 5) yes 6) The Boat Book   **Scanning:** 1) 6 2) 7 3) 5 4) 2

PAGE 17   **Completion:** 1) good 2) paper 3) book 4) read 5) make 6) boat   **Choose the Word:** 1) book 2) play 3) paper 4) good   **Sequencing:** 1-2-3

PAGE 18   **Yes/No:** 1) no 2) yes 3) no 4) yes 5) yes 6) yes 7) yes 8) no 9) no 10) no 11) yes 12) yes

PAGE 19   **Questions:** 1) The Cat on the Bus 2) white 3) school 4) boy 5) yes   **Scanning:** 1) 7 2) 1 3) 11 4) 7

PAGE 20   **Completion:** 1) wants 2) bus 3) white 4) cat 5) school   **Choose the Word:** 1) white 2) school 3) bus 4) cat 5) school   **Sequencing:** 2-3-1

PAGE 21   **Yes/No:** 1) yes 2) yes 3) yes 4) no 5) no 6) yes 7) yes 8) no 9) yes 10) no 11) yes 12) yes

PAGE 22   **Questions:** 1) bread 2) fox 3) bread 4) no 5) yes 6) The Chicken and the Bread

PAGE 23   **Scanning:** 1) 7 2) 10 3) 12 4) 9   **Completion:** 1) chicken 2) eat 3) ate 4) fox 5) fat
  Choose the Word: 1) yellow 2) fox 3) eat 4) fat 5) bread 6) did not

PAGE 24   **Sequencing:** 2-1-3   **Yes/No:** 1) yes 2) yes 3) no 4) yes 5) yes 6) yes 7) no 8) yes 9) no 10) yes

PAGE 25   **Questions:** 1) blue 2) by a puppy 3) ran away with it 4) ball 5) ball 6) The Boy and the Cap

Answer Key - Sight Word Stories and Seatwork Activities 1 (cont.)

PAGE 26   **Scanning:** 1) 7 2) 8 3) 7 4) 7   **Completion:** 1) like 2) cap 3) friend 4) puppy 5) boy 6) ball
                Choose the Word: 1) ball 2) blue 3) puppy 4) ran 5) ball 6) cap

PAGE 27   **Sequencing:** 2-3-1   **Yes/No:** 1) yes 2) no 3) yes 4) no 5) yes 6) yes 7) yes 8) no 9) yes 10) yes

PAGE 28   **Questions:** 1) The Green Car 2) green 3) on the grass 4) some men 5) black 6) on the street

PAGE 29   **Scanning:** 1) 4 2) 3 3) 11 4) 5 5) 1 6) 8   **Completion:** 1) not 2) men 3) car 4) man 5) street 6) drive
                Choose the Word: 1) big 2) grass 3) men, grass 4) black

PAGE 30   **Sequencing:** 1-2-3   **Yes/No:** 1) yes 2) no 3) yes 4) yes 5) no 6) yes 7) yes 8) yes 9) yes 10) yes

PAGE 31   **Questions:** 1) The Children and Their Coats 2) a joke 3) funny, home

PAGE 32   **Scanning:** 1) 11 2) 1 3) 7 4) 8 5) 2 6) 4   **Completion:** 1) children 2) joke 3) class 4) coat 5) right 6) tall
                Choose the Word: 1) play 2) boy 3) short 4) funny 5) mothers

PAGE 33   **Sequencing:** 3-1-2   **Yes/No:** 1) yes 2) yes 3) yes 4) yes 5) yes 6) yes 7) yes 8) no 9) yes 10) yes

PAGE 34   **Questions:** 1) Corn on the Road 2) something to eat 3) cake 4) bread 5) corn

PAGE 35   **Scanning:** 1) 4 2) 7 3) 3 4) 2 5) 2   **Completion:** 1) dog 2) road 3) cow 4) corn 5) farm 6) eat
                Choose the Word: 1) dog 2) road 3) cow 4) ate 5) bread

PAGE 36   **Sequencing:** 2-1-3   **Yes/No:** 1) yes 2) no 3) no 4) yes 5) yes 6) yes 7) no 8) yes 9) no 10) yes